# 300 Weird Spooky Facts About Halloween

Strange, Creepy, and Fun Facts to Get You in the Halloween Spirit!

**ARTER**

Copyright © 2024 by A. Arter. All rights reserved. No part of this publication may be reproduced, distributed, or transmitted in any form or by any means, including photocopying, recording, or other electronic or mechanical methods, without the prior permission of the publisher, except for brief quotations incorporated in reviews and other non-commercial uses permitted by copyright law.

# Introduction

If you love all things creepy, funny, and totally bizarre, then you're in for a treat (no tricks, we promise)! This book is packed with spooky and weird facts about Halloween that'll make you gasp, laugh, and maybe even shiver a little. From how people used to celebrate hundreds of years ago to the wild things we do today, these facts will take you on a fun and freaky ride through everything Halloween.

Why do we carve pumpkins? What's the deal with black cats? And how did candy become the star of the show?

Whether you're dressing up, telling ghost stories, or just love the spooky vibes, these 300 facts are perfect for sharing with friends, family, or anyone who loves Halloween as much as you do.

So, grab your favorite candy, get cozy, and let's dive into the weird, spooky, and sometimes hilarious world of Halloween!

# Here are 300 facts about Halloween:

1. The word "Halloween" means "hallowed evening" or "holy night."
2. Jack-o'-lanterns were originally carved from turnips, not pumpkins!
3. Black cats are often considered spooky, but in some countries, they are a sign of good luck.
4. Halloween is the second most popular holiday in the U.S., after Christmas.
5. People used to wear animal skins and heads as costumes to scare away evil spirits.

6. A fear of Halloween is called *Samhainophobia*.
7. The first jack-o'-lanterns were said to scare away ghosts.
8. Pumpkins come in many colors – orange, white, green, and even blue!
9. The world record for the largest pumpkin was 2,624 pounds. That's as heavy as a car!
10. Trick-or-treating started in the Middle Ages when people would dress up and beg for food.
11. Halloween comes from the ancient Celtic festival called *Samhain*.

12. Bobbing for apples was once a way to predict your future love!
13. In some places, it's believed seeing a spider on Halloween means a loved one is watching over you.
14. The largest Halloween parade is in New York City.
15. Bats are a popular Halloween symbol because they're active at night, like spooky creatures.
16. The first mention of "trick-or-treating" in the U.S. was in 1927.
17. Some people believe witches can turn into black cats.

18. If you wear your clothes inside out and walk backward on Halloween, you might see a witch!
19. Mexico celebrates a similar holiday called "Day of the Dead" (Día de los Muertos).
20. Candy corn was originally called "Chicken Feed" and wasn't meant to be Halloween candy.
21. People spend billions of dollars on Halloween candy every year!
22. The owl is a Halloween symbol because in medieval times, people thought owls were witches.

23. The largest haunted house in the world is in Lewisburg, Ohio – it's in a cave!
24. "Monster Mash" is a popular Halloween song that was released in 1962.
25. Halloween wasn't always a holiday for kids – it was originally for adults!
26. The first Halloween card was made in the early 1900s.
27. Some people still believe that ghosts roam the Earth on Halloween night.

28. It's said that if you hear footsteps behind you on Halloween, it could be a ghost!
29. The most popular Halloween candy is Reese's Peanut Butter Cups.
30. Ireland is considered the birthplace of Halloween.
31. Pumpkins are fruits, not vegetables!
32. Halloween is also called All Hallows' Eve.
33. Full moons on Halloween are rare, but super spooky when they happen!

34. The tradition of dressing up for Halloween comes from ancient people trying to blend in with spirits.
35. Candy corn has been around for more than 100 years!
36. "The Addams Family" and "The Munsters" are two famous Halloween-themed TV shows.
37. The fear of bats is called *Chiroptophobia*.
38. Skeletons are a Halloween symbol because they represent the dead.
39. Orange and black are Halloween colors because orange represents

harvest and black represents death.

40. In Alabama, it's illegal to dress up as a priest for Halloween.
41. Harry Houdini, the famous magician, died on Halloween in 1926.
42. Halloween candy sales are higher than Valentine's Day candy sales.
43. Some people believed ringing bells on Halloween would scare away evil spirits.
44. In the 1800s, Halloween was mostly about pulling pranks and causing mischief!

45. Candy wasn't given out on Halloween until the 1950s.
46. The most popular Halloween costume for pets is a pumpkin.
47. In the old days, people carved faces in vegetables to keep away ghosts.
48. The longest haunted house in the world is over 3,000 feet long.
49. Chocolate bars make up about 70% of all Halloween candy sales.
50. A blue pumpkin bucket means the child collecting candy might have autism.

51. Spiders are creepy Halloween creatures because they weave webs and live in dark places.
52. In the 1800s, people used to play pranks like throwing cabbages at houses.
53. The tradition of making lanterns from pumpkins started in the U.S.
54. Dracula is one of the most famous Halloween monsters.
55. Some people in Scotland used to throw nuts into the fire to see who they would marry.
56. You're more likely to see a ghost on Halloween, some believe,

because the "veil" between worlds is thin.
57. Glow sticks are a safe way to light up the night on Halloween.
58. Around 600 million pounds of candy are sold for Halloween every year.
59. There are more vampire legends than any other kind of monster story.
60. Some believe carving a jack-o'-lantern can help protect your home from spirits.
61. In Hollywood, there's a cemetery where famous stars are buried

called the "Hollywood Forever Cemetery."

62. The most popular Halloween costume for adults is a witch.

63. Halloween used to be called "Cabbage Night" in some parts of the U.S.

64. Some people believe you can tell the future by looking into a mirror at midnight on Halloween.

65. The fear of cemeteries is called *Coimetrophobia*.

66. Halloween was brought to America by Irish immigrants in the 1800s.

67. The fear of ghosts is called *Phasmophobia*.
68. Candy corn is made mostly of sugar, corn syrup, and marshmallow.
69. The movie *Hocus Pocus* has become a Halloween classic!
70. People once believed dressing as a ghost on Halloween could fool real spirits.
71. Scarecrows are a Halloween symbol because they remind us of harvest time.
72. You can roast pumpkin seeds for a tasty Halloween snack.

73. Some dogs and cats don't like wearing Halloween costumes because they feel uncomfortable.
74. If you see a bat flying around on Halloween, some people say it means ghosts are near!
75. Halloween is the busiest night of the year for haunted houses.
76. Vampires are popular Halloween monsters because of their spooky legend of drinking blood.
77. The fear of witches is called *Wiccaphobia*.
78. People use to believe witches could control the weather.

79. Pumpkins were once believed to be magical and could chase away evil spirits.
80. In some countries, people leave food out for wandering ghosts on Halloween night.
81. Black cats were once thought to be witches in disguise.
82. The fear of skeletons is called *Skeletophobia*.
83. Some people light bonfires on Halloween to keep spirits away.
84. In Italy, Halloween is not as big, but they celebrate something similar called *All Saints' Day*.

85. It's said that ghosts can't cross over running water, like rivers or streams.
86. Some people believe putting salt around your house can keep evil spirits away.
87. In Japan, they celebrate something similar to Halloween called *Obon*, where they honor ancestors.
88. Candy companies make Halloween-themed candies, like chocolate eyeballs!
89. The fear of clowns is called *Coulrophobia* – and it's a popular fear on Halloween.

90. Some people still make homemade costumes instead of buying them.
91. The scariest haunted house in the U.S. is called *McKamey Manor*, and you need to sign a waiver to go inside!
92. The fear of spiders is called *Arachnophobia*.
93. Witches are one of the oldest Halloween symbols, going back hundreds of years.
94. It's bad luck to see a black cat cross your path on Halloween, according to superstition.

95. Full moons are considered extra spooky on Halloween because they light up the night.
96. Some haunted houses are so scary, they make people sign a contract before entering.
97. If you hear an owl on Halloween, it's said to be a sign that something spooky is nearby!
98. Some people believe that throwing salt over your left shoulder will keep away evil spirits.
99. Halloween used to be called "All Hallow's Eve."
100. The fear of dolls is called *Pediophobia*.

101. In some places, people believe blowing out a jack-o'-lantern before midnight is bad luck.
102. It's said that ringing a bell on Halloween can scare away spirits.
103. The fear of blood is called *Hemophobia*.
104. The movie *Frankenstein* was based on a book written over 200 years ago!
105. Pumpkins are native to North America.
106. If you want to see a ghost, some people believe you should look through a keyhole at midnight.

107. The longest time to carve a pumpkin underwater is 3 minutes and 9 seconds!
108. There's a place in Ohio called "Pumpkinville" where they celebrate Halloween all year.
109. In Mexico, skeletons are a fun and happy symbol for *Día de los Muertos*.
110. People in some countries carve scary faces into melons instead of pumpkins.
111. The fear of vampires is called *Sanguivoriphobia*.
112. Halloween costumes used to be much scarier and homemade!

113. Mummies became a popular Halloween monster after ancient Egyptian tombs were discovered.
114. Some people believed the Northern Lights were ghosts dancing in the sky.
115. If you catch a falling leaf on Halloween, it's said to bring good luck.
116. The fear of fog is called *Homichlophobia*.
117. A "Harvest Moon" happens in the fall and is an extra bright full moon.
118. Haunted houses make over $300 million in the U.S. every Halloween.

119. Some people believe candles in jack-o'-lanterns guide lost spirits home.
120. Halloween decorations are a big business – Americans spend about $9 billion on them!
121. The fear of thunder and lightning is called *Astraphobia*.
122. Bats use echolocation to find their way in the dark, making them even spookier!
123. Some people believe sprinkling sage can cleanse an area of bad spirits.
124. There are more than 2,000 haunted houses in the U.S.

125. The fear of darkness is called *Nyctophobia*.
126. Ghost stories are a popular part of Halloween because people love to be scared.
127. Frankenstein's monster is often confused with his creator, Dr. Frankenstein.
128. Some people wear garlic on Halloween to keep vampires away.
129. It's said that if you stare into a mirror at midnight on Halloween, you might see a ghost.
130. The fear of zombies is called *Kinemortophobia*.

131. Dracula is based on a real person named Vlad the Impaler!
132. Halloween parties date back to the 1800s.
133. Haunted hotels are a popular attraction around Halloween.
134. The fear of being buried alive is called *Taphophobia*.
135. In some parts of the world, people go "ghost hunting" on Halloween.
136. The fear of ghosts is called *Spectrophobia*.
137. Pumpkins are 90% water!
138. Some people use black salt to protect against evil spirits.

139. A group of witches is called a coven.
140. In England, people used to make "soul cakes" on Halloween to give to the poor.
141. There's a town in Kansas named "Witchita," which sounds a lot like "witch"!
142. Halloween candy started being mass-produced in the 1950s.
143. If a candle in your jack-o'-lantern goes out by itself, it's considered a bad omen.
144. The fear of being scared is called *Phobophobia*.

145. The fear of cemeteries is called *Necrophobia*.
146. In Japan, people celebrate Halloween by wearing cute or funny costumes instead of scary ones.
147. The fear of werewolves is called *Lycanthropy*.
148. It's said that seeing a shooting star on Halloween means a ghost is near.
149. Some schools have "Black-and-Orange" days instead of Halloween parties.
150. Halloween used to be called "Snap Apple Night" in parts of the U.K. because of apple games!

151. There's a Halloween parade in West Hollywood where over 500,000 people show up!
152. Mummies were believed to have magical powers in ancient Egypt.
153. The world's fastest pumpkin carving took just 16.47 seconds!
154. Some Halloween masks glow in the dark to look even creepier at night.
155. Witches used to be thought of as helpful healers before becoming scary Halloween figures.
156. The tradition of telling ghost stories on Halloween night dates back centuries.

157. Some vampires in legends can turn into bats!
158. Candy wasn't always the treat given out on Halloween; sometimes people handed out toys.
159. Some places believe that putting a broom outside your door on Halloween keeps witches away.
160. It's said that if you laugh loudly on Halloween night, you can scare ghosts away.
161. You can tell how old a pumpkin is by counting the number of lines on its skin.

162. Dracula's castle, also called Bran Castle, is a real place in Romania!
163. The longest lasting jack-o'-lantern was lit for 41 days straight!
164. "Trick or treat, smell my feet" is a popular Halloween rhyme that kids like to chant.
165. In the olden days, it was common to play tricks like hiding people's farm equipment on Halloween.
166. The name Dracula means "son of the dragon."

167. Some countries have Halloween traditions where people leave out milk and bread for spirits.
168. Halloween used to be a time when people thought you could communicate with the dead.
169. Pumpkins float in water because they're 90% water!
170. The fear of clowns became more common because of scary clown movies.
171. Halloween wasn't very popular in the U.S. until the 1900s.
172. Some people believe that if a bat flies three times around your house

on Halloween, someone in the house will die.

173. "Bloody Mary" is a popular Halloween game where people believe a ghost will appear in the mirror.

174. Some people carve watermelon instead of pumpkins for fun jack-o'-lanterns!

175. Some people in the past believed witches could make themselves invisible.

176. Halloween is a great time to tell urban legends, like the story of the vanishing hitchhiker.

177. Apples were once used to predict who you would marry.
178. Halloween decorations used to be more homemade before stores sold spooky items.
179. Vampires can't see themselves in mirrors according to legends.
180. The candy industry makes around $2 billion a year just from Halloween!
181. It's said that burning a candle in your window on Halloween can guide lost spirits.
182. The most popular Halloween costume for kids in 2023 was Spider-Man!

183. There's a belief that witches can control animals like wolves and snakes.
184. Some people believed witches flew on broomsticks to meet other witches.
185. Halloween used to be called "Punkie Night" in some parts of England.
186. The most popular Halloween movie is *Hocus Pocus*!
187. Pumpkin patches are a popular place to visit during Halloween season.
188. Some haunted houses have mazes made of hay or corn stalks.

189. Owls are another popular Halloween symbol because they're nocturnal, just like bats.
190. In some countries, Halloween is celebrated over multiple days.
191. The fear of ghosts is one of the most common Halloween-related phobias.
192. The original vampire stories came from Eastern Europe.
193. Some people believed carrying a silver coin could protect you from vampires.
194. Witches were once thought to cast spells with the help of cats, especially black cats.

195. Halloween was once called "Nutcrack Night" because people would crack nuts by the fire.
196. There's a town in Canada called "Pumpkinhead"!
197. In some places, it's believed that walking backward on Halloween night confuses ghosts.
198. Some people believed sprinkling salt around your bed kept ghosts from haunting your dreams.
199. The movie *The Nightmare Before Christmas* is both a Halloween and a Christmas movie!

200. A bonfire used to be lit during Halloween to scare away evil spirits.
201. Halloween candy comes in special spooky shapes like ghosts and pumpkins.
202. Some ancient people believed witches brewed potions from weird ingredients like frog legs.
203. Vampires are often afraid of sunlight because it can kill them in most legends.
204. Some countries don't celebrate Halloween but have similar holidays honoring the dead.

205. The Guinness World Record for most people dressed as ghosts at once is over 560!
206. Halloween night is often considered the best time to perform spooky magic tricks.
207. Pumpkins are a type of squash.
208. Some haunted houses use fake fog to make them extra eerie.
209. The fear of witches and witchcraft is called *Wiccaphobia*.
210. Spooky cobwebs are used as Halloween decorations to make places look abandoned.

211. People in the past believed vampires could be stopped with garlic.
212. Halloween stores often sell fake blood to make costumes look scarier.
213. The biggest Halloween pumpkin festival is in Keene, New Hampshire.
214. Scarecrows were originally used to scare away birds from crops, not ghosts.
215. The first full-length Halloween movie was *Halloween* in 1978.
216. Ghost ships are a common theme in Halloween stories.

217. Some people dress up their cars for Halloween as part of "Trunk-or-Treat."
218. "Mischief Night" is the night before Halloween, when pranks used to happen.
219. The longest recorded haunted house experience is about 10 hours long!
220. Some cultures believe making noise at midnight on Halloween scares away spirits.
221. The fear of being buried alive is a real thing for some people!
222. Halloween can also be a time to honor pets that have passed away.

223. Some animals like owls and bats are called "Halloween animals" because of their nighttime habits.
224. In ancient Rome, people would celebrate the dead with a festival called *Lemuria*.
225. Pumpkin-flavored everything becomes popular during Halloween, including ice cream and candy.
226. Scary movies are a big tradition during Halloween, with marathons on TV all day long.
227. Some people believe that cemeteries are extra spooky on Halloween night.

228. Many Halloween superstitions involve mirrors, like seeing ghosts in them.
229. Spooky haunted hayrides are popular around Halloween.
230. The tradition of wearing masks for Halloween came from trying to confuse spirits.
231. In some places, trick-or-treating is done in malls or parks instead of neighborhoods.
232. In Spain, they bake special cakes called *Huesos de Santo* (Saint's Bones) for Halloween.
233. Bats can eat up to 1,000 insects in an hour!

234. The first vampire movie was called *Nosferatu* and came out in 1922.
235. In the Philippines, kids go door-to-door during *Pangangaluluwa* to sing and ask for alms.
236. Some cultures believe ghosts can get trapped in mirrors if they aren't covered.
237. Some Halloween parties feature "spooky karaoke" with songs like "Thriller."
238. Some haunted houses are set up in real haunted places!
239. The fear of skeletons is called *Skeletophobia*.

240. Popular Halloween snacks include caramel apples and popcorn balls.
241. Candy apples are sometimes called "Toffee Apples" in other countries.
242. The first haunted house attractions started in the 1930s.
243. You can turn pumpkins into pies, soups, and even bread!
244. There's a vampire museum in New Orleans!
245. Some people dress up as their favorite superheroes for Halloween instead of spooky costumes.

246. Candles are often used in Halloween decorations because they create spooky shadows.
247. Witches are often shown stirring cauldrons full of bubbling green goo.
248. The most expensive Halloween costume ever made cost over $1 million!
249. There's a fear of Halloween called *Samhainophobia*.
250. In some places, Halloween is all about giving instead of getting, with people handing out food to the poor.

251. Some people believe that hearing an owl hoot three times on Halloween night is a bad omen.
252. Candy buckets come in all kinds of fun shapes, like pumpkins, ghosts, and bats.
253. Some people believed that if you didn't dress up on Halloween, ghosts would follow you home.
254. Halloween parties often have games like "Pin the Tail on the Black Cat."
255. A "vampire bat" is a real species of bat that feeds on blood.
256. In ancient times, people used to celebrate Halloween by lighting

huge bonfires to ward off evil spirits.

257. Some schools hold Halloween costume contests for the funniest or scariest outfits.

258. The tradition of wearing black on Halloween represents death and the unknown.

259. Halloween is the perfect time to play pranks on your friends and family!

260. Fake cobwebs are popular Halloween decorations that make homes look abandoned and creepy.

261. Skeleton decorations are used because they remind people of the dead.
262. Some legends say vampires can only enter your house if you invite them in.
263. Wearing masks on Halloween was believed to keep you safe from wandering spirits.
264. Pumpkins used for jack-o'-lanterns were once believed to scare away evil spirits.
265. If you leave out food for ghosts on Halloween night, some people believe it brings good luck.

266. Halloween is a time when many people try to communicate with the spirits of loved ones.
267. Some believe throwing a stone into a bonfire on Halloween can help you see your future.
268. Halloween isn't just for kids; adults love dressing up and going to spooky parties too!
269. Halloween piñatas filled with candy are a fun way to celebrate.
270. Many places host "ghost tours" to show people around haunted areas.

271. Carving pumpkins into funny faces is just as popular as making them scary!
272. Pumpkin seeds can be roasted and eaten as a yummy Halloween snack.
273. The fastest time to carve a pumpkin blindfolded is 1 minute and 42 seconds!
274. A Halloween costume trend is to dress as characters from popular movies.
275. Pumpkin-flavored candy and drinks get super popular in October.

276. Some pumpkins grow to be over 1,000 pounds and are entered into competitions.
277. In some parts of the world, people don't celebrate Halloween at all!
278. Some people still go "apple bobbing" at Halloween parties.
279. The largest gathering of people dressed as witches was 1,607!
280. Orange and black are the traditional Halloween colors.
281. People sometimes play hide-and-seek in the dark for a spooky twist on the game.

282. Ghost tours often visit old, creepy buildings and tell haunted stories.
283. Halloween makes up about 10% of the entire candy industry's yearly sales.
284. "Trunk or treat" events let kids go trick-or-treating from car to car in parking lots.
285. The first vampire bats were discovered in South America.
286. People used to carve scary faces into turnips before pumpkins became popular.

287. Skeletons are often shown dancing in spooky cartoons and decorations.
288. In Germany, people hide knives on Halloween night to keep ghosts from using them.
289. Some families carve jack-o'-lanterns as a yearly tradition, with each person making their own design.
290. Some haunted houses have actors who jump out to scare you!
291. In Ireland, people used to celebrate Halloween by having bonfires and telling scary stories.

292. Some people have Halloween movie marathons where they watch scary films all night long.
293. Chocolate bars are one of the most popular Halloween treats.
294. Some Halloween costumes light up in the dark, making them look extra cool!
295. Scary music is often played at Halloween parties to set a spooky mood.
296. Fake spiders and skeletons are common Halloween decorations.
297. Some people host Halloween scavenger hunts with spooky prizes.

298. Black cats are often shown in Halloween stories and decorations because they are believed to be mysterious.
299. Corn mazes become a popular activity during Halloween time.
300. Halloween is the second biggest holiday for decorations after Christmas!

And there you have it – 300 weird, spooky, and totally awesome Halloween facts!

By now, you've discovered some of the wildest things about Halloween, from ancient traditions to modern-day scares. Whether you're a fan of creepy costumes, haunted houses, or just love candy, Halloween is full of surprises and fun.

Remember, Halloween isn't just about being scared – it's about having a good time, getting creative, and maybe learning a thing or two along the way. Hopefully, these facts have made you laugh, say "Whoa, that's crazy!" or even give your friends some fun trivia to share at the next Halloween party.

So, next time you put on a costume, carve a pumpkin, or tell a ghost story, think about all the spooky, weird, and cool things that make Halloween one of the best holidays ever!

Until next time, stay spooky, have fun, and keep the Halloween spirit alive all year long!

Made in the USA
Monee, IL
25 October 2024

68662585R00035